Great Garden Quotes

A COLORING BOOK
WITH WIT, WISDOM,
& HEART

From the Pages of

GreenPrints
"The Weeder's Digest"

GreenPrints
Enterprises

Great Garden Quotes
A Coloring Book of Wit, Wisdom, & Heart
Edited by Pat Stone

Published by GreenPrints Enterprises, Inc. *www.greenprints.com*
Copyright ©2016 by GreenPrints Enterprises, Inc. All Rights Reserved.

ISBN   978-0-692-76226-4 (pbk.)

Cover Design by Sandie Rhodes
Cover Art by Dena Seiferling
Back Cover Art by Blanche Derby (dog), P. Savage (car and man), Heather
Graham (mailbox)
Art this page by Heather Graham
Special Thanks to Betty MacKey for hours and hours of art-unshading toil

Printed in the United States of America by Sheridan Press

Welcome!

Welcome, indeed, to the most beautiful, fun, and inspiring coloring book ever created (Pat says modestly). How can I make such a, uh, colorful claim?

1. Because it's about *gardening*, the most beautiful, fun, and inspiring outdoor activity of all (as every gardener knows).

2. Because the art and quotes herein have been collected *over 26 years*! The art was created by an array of talented illustrators from all over North America and originally published in issues of my magazine, GREENPRINTS, *"The Weeder's Digest"* (more about GREENPRINTS at the end of this book).

I've had great fun collecting and sharing this stunning array of gorgeous, moving, and lighthearted art over the decades.

And now you get to have great fun coloring them in (and removing them and framing them if you wish).

Enjoy and Happy Gardening!

Pat Stone, Editor
GREENPRINTS, *"The Weeder's Digest"*

P.S. In fairness to the original artists, I'd like to note that, to make the pages more fun to color, we've had to unshade and decolor many of these illustrations. Sometimes this has made a drawing less beautiful than it was originally (compare the art on your left with that on p. 67, for instance). That's all right. By the time you're done coloring, I'm sure they'll look even better than before!

Artist Credits

I want to very, very gratefully thank all the wonderful illustrators whose work is included here. Your gifts of art bring our magazine to life.
— Pat

Flowers are the sweetest things God ever made
and forgot to put a soul into.
—Henry Ward Beecher

With a garden there is hope.
—Grace Firth

A real garden where one can enter in
and forget the whole world
cannot be made in a week or a month or a year.
It must be planned for and waited for
and loved into being.
—Chinese Proverb

What a man needs in gardening
is a cast-iron back
with a hinge in it.
—Charles Dudley Warner

You don't have a garden just for yourself.
You have it to share.
—Augusta Carter

*I do sincerely trust that the benediction
that is always awaiting me in my garden may
by degrees be more deserved, and that I may grow
in grace, and patience, and cheerfulness, just like
the happy flowers I so much love.*
—Elizabeth von Armin

A bit of fragrance always clings
to the hands that give roses.
—Chinese Proverb

What continues to astonish me about a garden
is that you can walk past it in a hurry,
see something wrong, stop to set it right,
and emerge an hour or two later
breathless, contented, and wondering
what on earth happened.
—Dorothy Gilman

Earth laughs in flowers.
—Ralph Waldo Emerson

Delicate snow-drop
with a thrust of purest steel
you pierce last year's leaves.
　　　　—Rosemary Hyman

To see a thing in a seed,
that is genius.
—Lau Tzu

It's spring fever. That is what the name of it is.
And when you've got it, you want—
oh, you don't quite know what it is you do want,
but it just fairly makes your heart ache,
you want it so!
—Mark Twain

The

Gardener

in his old brown hands
Turns over the brown earth,
As if he loves and understands
The flowers before their birth.

Arthur Symons

*I love spring anywhere, but if I could choose
I would always greet it in a garden.*
—Ruth Stout

First a howling blizzard woke us,
Then the rain came down to soak us,
And now before the eye can focus—
Crocus.

—Lilja Rogers

He that plants trees
loves others besides himself.
— Thomas Fuller

A spring day
feeds a whole year.
—Russian Proverb

If I could put my words in song,
And tell what's there enjoyed,
All men would to my gardens throng,
And leave the cities void.
—Ralph Waldo Emerson

When at last I took the time
to look into the heart of a flower,
it opened up a whole new world . . .
as if a window had been opened
to let in the sun.
—Princess Grace Kelly

A garden is one of those pernicious machineries
which catch a man's coat-skirt or his hand,
and draw in his arm, his leg, and his whole
body to irresistible destruction.
—Ralph Waldo Emerson

Birds are flowers flying
and flowers perched birds.

—A. R. Ammons

The beauty, the grandeur, the faithfulness of my garden.
Despite the miseries of the times, my garden, what don't I owe
to you? Despite the atrocities of man, because of you
I will have kept a little happiness, a little faith, a little dignity.
I will have lived, thanks to you, a life always new, always dependable
and comforting, close to the living things in the universe.
—Fernand Lequenna

People from a planet without flowers would think
we must be mad with joy the whole time
to have such things about us.
—Iris Murdoch

A garden is a thing of beauty
and a job forever.
—Anonymous

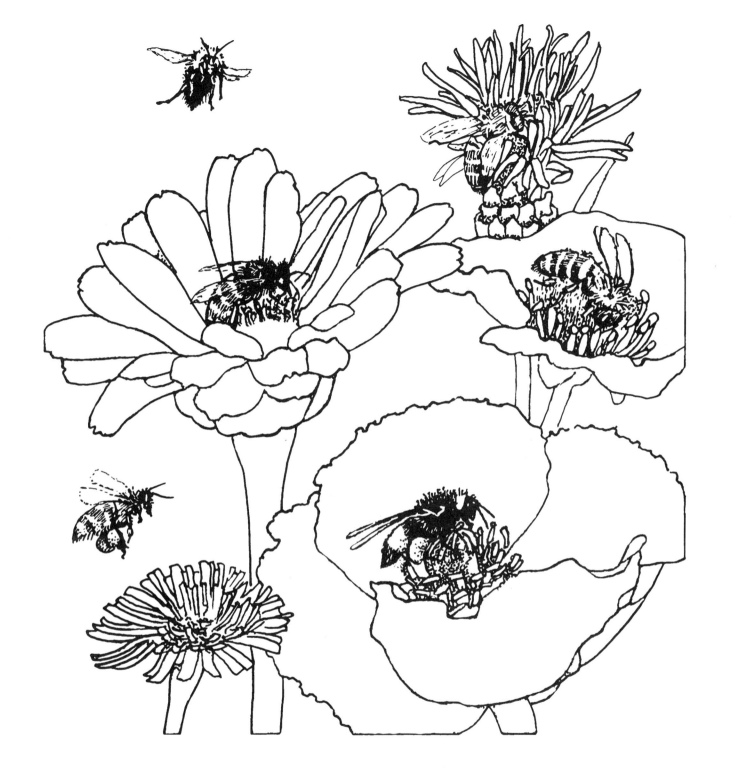

Bees do have a smell, you know,
and if they don't they should,
for their feet are dusted with spices
from a million flowers.
—Ray Bradbury

*Sweet flowers are slow
and weeds make haste.*
—William Shakespeare

I don't know how people deal with their moods when they have no garden, raspberry patch, or field to work in. You can take your angers, frustrations, bewilderments to the earth, working savagely, working up a sweat and an ache and a great weariness. The work rinses out the cup of your spirit, leaves it washed and clean and ready to be freshly filled with new hope. It is one of the reasons I am addicted to raspberry patches. The pie is purely symbolic.
—Rachel Penden

Some people have lots of flowers,
some people have lots of pets.
But nobody has lots of pets and lots of flowers.
—Sally Roth

A vegetable garden in the beginning
looks so promising and then after all
little by little it grows nothing but
vegetables, nothing, nothing but vegetables.
—Gertrude Stein

It is not enough
for the gardener to love flowers.
He must also hate weeds.
—Anonymous

To laugh often and much; to win the respect
of intelligent people and the affection of children;
to earn the appreciation of honest critics, and
endure the betrayal of false friends; to appreciate
beauty, to find the best in others; to leave the
world a bit better, whether by a healthy child,
a garden patch or a redeemed social condition;
to know even one life has breathed easier because
you lived. That is to have succeeded.
—Ralph Waldo Emerson

Flowers
are the poor
man's poetry.
-Anne Pratt

Gardening is a knife edge between
disaster and serendipity.
—Jinny Blom

What I'd like to express
is this simple affirmation:
Growing, harvesting, cooking, and eating
something that you've grown
—no matter how tiny the yield—
is one of the most important and
nearly lost of human art forms.
—Stephen Orr

Since the best way of weeding
Is to prevent weeds from seeding,
The least procrastination
Of any operation
To prevent the semination
Of noxious vegetation
Is a source of tribulation.
And this, in truth, a fact is
Which gardeners out to practice
And tillers should remember
From April to December.
                    —New England Farmer, 1829

Flowers always make people
better, happier, and more helpful;
they are sunshine, food, and medicine to the soul.
—Luther Burbank

Who gardens with a clenched fist?
Gardens slow things down,
relax that death grip with which
we grasp the time we are given.
—Dominique Browning

One can get just as much exultation
in losing oneself in a little thing
as in a big thing. It is nice to think
how one can be recklessly lost
in a daisy.
—Anne Morrow Lindbergh

All gardeners live in beautiful places
because they made them so.
—Joseph Joubert

All my hurts
my garden spade can heal.
—Ralph Waldo Emerson

*Even if something is left undone, everyone must take
time to sit still and watch the leaves turn.*
—Elizabeth Lawrence

The true meaning of life
is to plant trees
under whose shade
you do not expect to sit.
—Helen Henderson

No shade, no shine, no butterflies, no bees,
no fruit, no flowers, no leaves, no buds,
November!
—Thomas Hood

When the world wearies and society ceases to satisfy,
there is always the garden.
—Minnie Aumonier

One must first seek to love plants and nature, and then to
cultivate that happy peace of mind which is satisfied with little.
He will be happier if he has no rigid and arbitrary ideals,
for gardens are coquettish, particularly with the novice.
—Liberty Hyde Bailey

A gardener is someone who thinks that
what goes down must come up.
—Author Unknown

Arranging a bowl of flowers in the morning
can give a sense of quiet in a crowded day
—like writing a poem, or saying a prayer.
—Anne Morrow Lindbergh

Gardeners spend half their time on their knees
and the other half trying to get up.
—Anonymous

In The Garden of Happy Memories,
It Is Always Summer.
—*Sign in an English Cottage Garden*

Dilettante's Holiday

The garden spreads across my day
like four pounds of Belgian chocolate
I will try every corner
finish nothing.

Anita Stamper

A garden is a lovely spot
At least that's true of the one we got
A lovely spot for weeds to grow in
And me to sweat and dig and hoe in
And kids to clobber balls and stones in
And neighbors' dogs to bury bones in
And aphids by the hordes to work in
And mealy bugs and slugs to work in
And soil to harden like cement in
And flowers to bloom by accident in.
—Anonymous

Man—despite his artistic pretensions,
his sophistication and his many accomplishments—
owes his existence to a six-inch layer of topsoil
and the fact that it rains.
—John Jeavons

Winter is in my head
But eternal spring is in my heart.
—Victor Hugo

*The garden must be prepared in the soul first
or else it will never flourish.*
—English Proverb

All the flowers of tomorrow
are in the seeds of today.
—Anonymous

In all the recipes for happiness I have ever seen,
"something to look forward to" has been given
as an important ingredient. Something to look forward to!
How rich the gardener, any gardener,
is in this particular ingredient!
—Louse Beebe Wilder

A garden in the winter
is a gift wrapped in snow.
—Anonymous

Take care of yourself.
The garden needs you.
—M.E. Keeble

*Look into a true gardener's eyes
and Eden shines through . . . small wonder,
for a garden feeds the soul.*
—Peter Ellenshaw

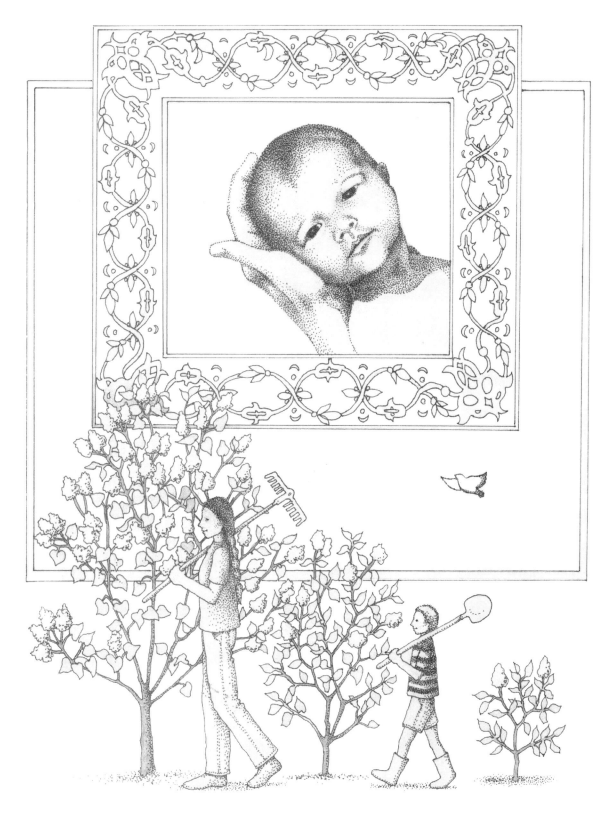

Gardening shouldn't be a grim business.
If you've forgotten that, it's time you learned
a lesson from your children.
—Richard Nichols

The garden suggests there might be a place
where we can meet nature halfway.
—Michael Pollan

Earth's crammed with heaven,
and every common bush afire with God.
—Elizabeth Barrett Browning

The trouble arises
(as it usually does in all fields of endeavor)
when you stop reading
and start doing.
—Henry Mitchell

"Flower in the crannied wall,
  I pluck you out of the crannies,
I hold you here, root and all, in my hand,
Little flower – but if I could understand
What you are, root and all, and all in all,
  I should know what God and man is."
                              Alfred Lord Tennyson

Love the things nearest at hand and love intensely.
If I were to write a motto over the gate of a garden,
I should choose the remark which Socrates made
as he saw the luxuries in the market, "How much
there is in the world that I do not want."
—Liberty Hyde Bailey

Our highest assurance of the goodness of Providence seems to me
to rest in the flowers. All other things, our powers, our desires,
our food, are all really necessary for our existence in the first instance.
But this rose is an extra. Its smell and its color are an embellishment
of life, not a condition of it. It is only goodness which gives extras,
and so I say again that we have much to hope from the flowers.
—Sir Arthur Conan Doyle

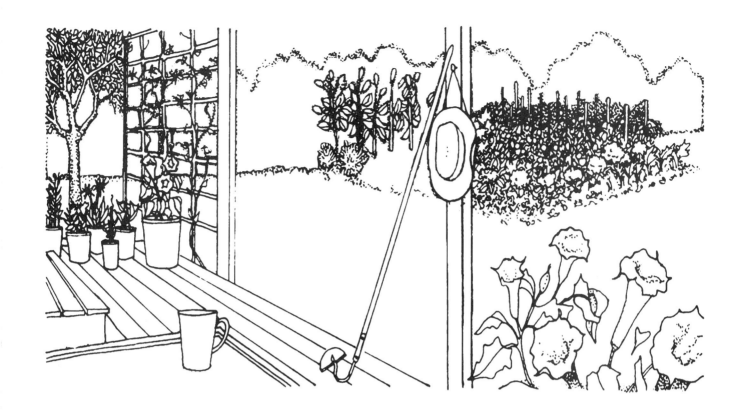

A Gardener's Blessing

May God grant thee
   Enough sun to warm the earth,
   Enough rain to make things grow,
   A good strong back,
   A wide-brimmed hat,
   And a good sharp goose-neck hoe,
   Strength for a day of toil,
   And some quiet evening hours,
   With a sip of tea
   And a gentle breeze,
   And may all your weeds be wildflowers.
         —Ralph Emerson Purkhiser

Do the best that you can
in the place where you are,
and be kind.
—Scott Nearing

WHAT

A Great Gardener's Gift!

No. 37 $6.00   SPRING 1999
GREENPRINTS
"THE WEEDER'S DIGEST"

"Wilbo!"
DOGS AND GARDENING

Our 27th Year!

And Now, Just in Case You've Been Wondering . . .

IS

No. 101 $6.00   SPRING 2015
GREENPRINTS
"THE WEEDER'S DIGEST"

25TH ANNIVERSARY YEAR!
P.14 LOOK
P.74 ARE PLANTS <u>SMART</u>?
P.26 LADYBUGS ON THE LOOSE!

GREENPRINTS, "The Weeder's Digest"?

No. 19 $6.00   AUTUMN 1996
GREENPRINTS
"THE WEEDER'S DIGEST"

WHO IS THE GREEN MAN?

* Get This Story FREE! See Back.

No. 48 $6.00   WINTER 2001
GREENPRINTS
"THE WEEDER'S DIGEST"

P.66 MY GARDEN, MY HEALER
P.12 CATALOG MUMBO-JUMBO
P.92 RANSACKED BY RABBITS

There are over 100 how-to gardening publications in this country. Only **GREENPRINTS** shares the joy, the humor, the headaches, and the heart in wonderful stories and beautiful art. It's the <u>personal</u> garden magazine.

HUMOR

My No-Grow Azaelas

Why, oh why, did they stop?

• • •

Several years ago, I planted eight azaleas to make a hedge alongside the house. Every spring they lit up our home with a beautiful display of dazzling white blossoms.

For the past three years, though, they hadn't gotten any bigger. It was as if all eight of them had suddenly decided to stop growing. My concerns were growing; my azaleas were not. It was time to take action. I started

- Quarterly • Full-Color Cover
- 80 Pages • Black-&-White Art
- 13 Stories (or more) Every Issue!
- Web Site: www.greenprints.com

"Before? I was leery it could be as good as your customer quotes say it is. After? When I stumbled in the driveway, my nose stuck in the magazine, I knew that I, too, was hooked!"
—Jane Barnard
S. Egremont, MA

The GreenPrints Story

For 12 years, I was the Garden Editor at Mother Earth News magazine. Each year, I told people how to prune their raspberries, plant their bulbs, and test their soil. After a while, I began to feel that I was neglecting the joys, the feelings, the experiences— the heart and soul of gardening. That's why I started GreenPrints. Not to instruct. Not to preach. But to share.

Pat Stone

Pat Stone, Editor
Co-Author, Chicken Soup for the Gardener's Soul

INSIGHT

The Story of St. Fiacre

The real patron saint of gardening.

♦ ♦ ♦

Saint Fiacre was a wildman of gardening, a miracle worker who bargained with the church, had problems with a witch, and became the patron saint of cab-drivers. His gardening miracle came about when

& HEART

One Million Daisies

Why I weed my mother's garden.

A million daisies have invaded my mother's garden. They grow rampant among the phlox and delphinium, the lilies and the roses. She doesn't want their scraggly disorder in her beds, but

GreenPrints • P.O. Box 1355 — www.greenprints.com — Fairview, NC 28730 • 800-569-0602

- -